# ALMOST CHRISTMAS

## A WESLEYAN ADVENT EXPERIENCE

MAGREY R. DEVEGA · INGRID MCINTYRE
APRIL CASPERSON · MATT RAWLE

DEVOTIONS FOR THE SEASON

Abingdon Press
Nashville

# Almost Christmas Devotions for the Season
## A Wesleyan Advent Experience

*Copyright © 2019 by Abingdon Press*
*All rights reserved.*

*Library of Congress Cataloging-in-Publication data has been requested.*
ISBN 978-1-5018-9069-7

19 20 21 22 23 24 25 26 27 28—10 9 8 7 6 5 4 3 2 1
MANUFACTURED IN THE UNITED STATES OF AMERICA

# CONTENTS

# Contents

# Introduction

Our Advent journey requires a road map, one that will orient us in the right direction and chart our progress. For this Advent, we turn to one of the most important sermons that John Wesley every preached.

It was on July 25, 1741, that John Wesley preached a sermon to his fellow Oxford University colleagues called "The Almost Christian," in which he described a person who, on the surface, had all the outward appearance of godliness. This person did all the basic things right: practiced decency toward others, went to church, abstained from bad behavior, and sincerely tried to do his or her best. But Wesley would say that as commendable as that person might be (and wouldn't it be great if everyone were at least that good!), such a person would only be *almost* a Christian.

Instead, Wesley called followers of Jesus to live an "altogether" life, one that, first of all, fully loves God: "Such a love is this," he writes, "as engrosses the whole heart, as rakes up all the affections, as fills the entire capacity of the soul and employs the utmost extent of all its faculties."[1] Second, he calls us to fully love others, including and especially those who have wronged us, and those whom we have wronged. Third, he calls us to have a full trust and confidence in God, so that the faith is not just an exercise in intellectual conviction, but a holistic offering of mind, body, and spirit. An "altogether" Christian is one who unreservedly and wholeheartedly trusts God and puts that trust into action.

To help his hearers and readers get from that *almost* faith to one that *altogether* loves God, Wesley's sermon is filled with dozens of questions. Each one explores a different aspect of a life that is fully committed to Jesus Christ, ranging from belief ("Do I believe that Jesus has taken away my sins and cast them as a stone into the depth of the sea?") to practice ("Do I seriously follow God's commandments whenever I can?") to our relationships with others ("Do I love others as Christ loved me?")

Even though "The Almost Christian" was never intended to be an Advent or Christmas sermon, its questions can still guide us in our Advent journey, especially in preparing us to receive Christ more fully in our hearts and lives. For the next thirty-one days, beginning on December 1, we invite you to explore each question in depth, interspersed with meditations on some popular Christmas carols. And we will conclude on December 31 with a reminder of the Wesley Covenant Prayer to prepare you for the new year.

Read each entry, pray through the questions that Wesley asks, and consider how God is leading you to make steady movement from an *almost* faith to an *altogether* one, as we welcome a fresh arrival of Jesus into our lives.

*Magrey R. deVega*

---

1 John Wesley, Sermon 2 "The Almost Christian," accessed July 21, 2019, http://wesley.nnu.edu/john-wesley/the-sermons-of-john-wesley-1872-edition/sermon-2-the-almost-christian/.

---

1

---

## Do I so far practice justice, mercy, and truth, as even the world requires?

On a recent trip to the local Starbucks, I encountered a couple who looked like they needed something. Actually it looked like they needed more than just something—they looked sad, wearied, and weak. As I passed them, my heart began tugging within me. Moments later I would learn more about them, as they soon called me over and explained their predicament.

Now I have to admit that this seems to happen to me often. I love meeting people and hearing their stories, and like a parent or grandparent I always want to be helpful to those I encounter. But sometimes, it is different. Sometimes, like this time, it is much more than a mere desire to be helpful. It is a certain conviction that I am looking straight into the eyes of Jesus.

As I sat with this couple, learned their names, and heard their story, the presence of Jesus became even clearer. They had not had a meal in a few days and all they wanted was a few dollars to get a little something at the convenience store across the street. I invited them to come in and have breakfast at Starbucks on me. They were both surprised; tears fell on their cheeks and gratitude came to the surface. We stood in line and ordered, and then waited patiently together. As we waited, we shared more stories of life, of how we ended up at Starbucks that day, and about our faith.

When their food arrived, I hugged each of them and we went our separate ways.

Whenever I tell this story or relate others like it, the same question comes up nearly every time: How do you know that you are actually helping a person, and that they are not just taking advantage of you?

As we begin this Advent journey of preparation, John Wesley gives us a different question—a simple yet profound one. "Do I so far practice justice, mercy, and truth, as even the world requires?" Or to put it another way, Do we practice justice, mercy, and truth at the most basic human level?

In the Sermon on the Mount, Jesus reminds us not to judge others. He challenges us to pay attention to our own attitudes and motivations and not to be so concerned with the failures of others. He then reminds us to ask for what we need: "If you who are evil know how to give good gifts to your children, how much more will your heavenly Father give good things to those who ask him" (Matthew 7:11). We can be bold to ask God for what we need, knowing that God will provide for what is best. Even earthly, non-perfect parents would do that.

We should take Jesus' teaching here to heart as an example of the justice, mercy, and truth that even the world requires. Even imperfect parents will respond to the need of a child in front of them.

Returning to the couple I met in Starbucks: How do I know that I'm not being taken advantage of? My response is that it doesn't matter. In fact, I don't know—there are no guarantees that I will give to an urgent need. But I do know that if I were in their situation, I would want to receive the help I need, the just thing, the merciful response, and the truth of the situation. That is how I would want anyone to approach me, so why would I not do the same? I can respond to the need in front of me, leaving the outcome to God.

As you begin this Advent journey, pay attention to the ways that God shows up in your life. Today at every possible moment do justice, practice mercy, and reveal truth in the most basic, easy, and human way. It is in this small step that our souls find renewal, that our hearts prepare to receive the Christ Child, and that others can see a star in the east.

Maybe this year Christ will be born in a Starbucks instead of a stable!

*Rev. Juan Huertas*

## 2

# Do I even appear on the outside to be a Christian?

During my senior year of college, I lived in a house my roommates and I called the Castle. One of the bedrooms had a spire for a ceiling! As graduation approached, I spent hours outside taking in the sun on a wooden swing hung from a large oak tree. One day when we were outside, my friend Sam and I began talking about postgraduation plans. Sam and I had previously been on the crew team together, so we knew each other fairly well. I told him about the Christian summer camp I was headed to work for, as I had done the previous two summers. After listening to my excitement and passion for Mountain T.O.P., Sam looked at me and said, "I didn't know you were a Christian."

There was a moment of hush as I gazed at Sam with disbelief. I was embarrassed and hurt. I thought to myself, "What!? I spend my summers working in ministry! I lead huge camps of people spiritually! I even preach!" As his observation swept over me in the hours that followed, I was mad at myself. Why didn't my life speak of my love for God?

As Christians, we are called to self-examination at every point of our spiritual journey. John Wesley's question, "Do I even appear on the outside to be a Christian," reminds us that what may feel and seem so obvious to us may not be expressed in our day-to-day actions. If we give our practice an honest and faithful look, God will help weave our beliefs and actions together even more tightly. This Advent, let us strive for our outward behaviors to reflect the hope and expectation we feel inside as we long for Christ's coming.

I'd had a completely opposite experience a few years before my conversation with Sam. When I returned from my first summer working at Mountain T.O.P., my friend Page said to me, "Something is different about you!" What Page saw was the fire and joy of a mountaintop experience. All summer I studied the Scripture and worshiped God under the stars. I listened to youth tell stories of hope and transformation. I watched children and families find shelter, friendship, and new life in partnership with these youth. And my own call to ordained ministry was being nurtured, as mentors and campers called out spiritual gifts God had planted in me.

One of the hardest tasks of a Christian is leaving worship, or a service trip, or a mountaintop experience. We experience that thin veil between heaven and earth and try to hold on to it as we reenter our worlds. Perhaps we feel it during Advent worship or among close friends and family at Christmas. Perhaps it's during service to others at this special time of the year that we feel God's nearness. Whatever it may be, we have to leave these places where we have tasted and seen that the Lord is good with the intention to practice daily positioning ourselves before God. When we create a space to encounter God, we are better able to live out that love as we rise and go out.

As we wear our encounters with God, as we wake up and clothe ourselves with the fruit of the Spirit, people will ask: Why are you so joyful? How are you so confident in times of sorrow? Our personal, sacred encounters become our everyday, ordinary witness. Our stories become our invitation into the redemptive and abundant life offered in Jesus Christ.

*Rev. Sam McGlothlin*

---

3

---

# Do I practice godly behavior?

When our children were born, one of the values we wanted to instill in them was deep empathy. The question we faced was, how do we teach our children to care deeply for those who are not like them? How do they learn to see and imagine what it might be like to be someone wholly different? Over the past decade, we have learned very different ways of practicing this value of empathy. One of our favorite practices is to fill gallon-sized resealable bags with items that we have learned over the years folks in our community both need and want. Clean socks, Starbucks gift cards, and healthy snacks are a few examples of things we have learned to pack in these bags after meeting people who are in need and sharing our names and stories. Something else we have learned is the value of writing notes and prayers that aren't patronizing, but rather focused on honoring the humanity and dignity in each person we meet.

When we reflect on John Wesley's question, "Do I practice godly behavior?" we do well if it leads us to practice empathy. One of the beautiful traits of the God we worship is that this God deeply empathizes with God's creation. So much so that God was emptied out for all of creation. Consider Paul's words in Philippians:

15

*Who, being in very nature God,*
    *did not consider equality with God something to be*
    *used to his own advantage;*
*rather, he made himself nothing*
    *by taking the very nature of a servant,*
    *being made in human likeness.*
*And being found in appearance as a man,*
    *he humbled himself*
    *by becoming obedient to death—*
        *even death on a cross!*

*(Philippians 2:6-8 NIV)*

In this Advent season, we worship God who leans in to who we are as creation as we seek God who loved us first. There are so many wonderful and challenging aspects of the behavior of God that we can read about in the Hebrew Scriptures and New Testament. One of the most powerful in my mind is God who came to us humbly, even as a newborn child, so we might love Jesus who walked the same paths we walk, suffered as we suffer, and loved perfectly.

In this season of Advent, what does it mean to you that God leans in to creation? God whose love manifested in Jesus the Christ? God whose behaviors are beyond our wisdom and yet whose actions of love and grace are known through his Son Jesus? How do God's actions challenge, encourage, and mold who you are today as you journey toward the wonderous birth of Jesus?

In this Advent season, we are called to personal holiness and reflection as we consider God's loving behavior for all of creation. We are also challenged to consider God's love beyond our individual needs and personal devotion. If your spiritual gallon bag were to be filled today, what would you place within it? Would you add items of comfort for those needing to experience God's presence? Would you focus on substance to feed those around you so they know your actions match your intentions? What would you write in each note to reflect the amazing grace God offers?

As you begin your day, I invite you to thank God for the many ways in which God leans in to us, loves us, and seeks us. Offer to God all that you are, and all that you might ever be, in the name of Jesus.

*Rev. DJ del Rosario*

## 4

# Do I refrain from doing evil things, as is described in the Bible?

I've often wondered: when Jesus was a toddler, did his mother have to teach him not to bite other children? Toddlers are some of the most violent humans on the planet. Most toddlers have to be taught not to bite or hit. They have to be taught to share.

Christians typically have one of two answers to this question. Some say, "Absolutely not! Jesus was sinless and perfectly loving. He would have been a sweet child, even as a toddler. The Holy Spirit would have directed him to always share and never hurt other children." Others, especially those who have been parents, are more circumspect. They say, "Of course he had to be taught not to bite. Learning is part of the human experience, and we can hardly say he was fully human if he didn't have to learn right from wrong."

I don't have an answer. The Bible is silent about Jesus' childhood, except for that one time he wandered off and his parents spent three days searching for him in Jerusalem. As far as childhood stories go, that sounds pretty normal for a precocious kid.

Our earliest training in ethics is pretty straightforward: "Thou shalt not." Don't hit. Don't bite. Don't throw objects in Grandma's dining room. Don't gossip or insult people. And when God brings freed slaves out of Egypt and gives them rules for living together, God gives them the Ten Commandments that often tell them what not to do. We might think of the Ten Commandments as the Israelite people's version of toddler ethics. Don't make graven images. Don't kill. Don't commit adultery. Don't covet. These are minimum-level rules for getting along as a society of diverse people with diverse motives and interests. Ethicists call this "deontological" or "rule-based" ethics.

As we mature, the lessons get more nuanced. We start asking why, and we begin to learn a version of ethics that goes beyond "thou shalt not" to a more positive vision of the world God wants. Why do we honor the sabbath? Because labor laws are important to keep people and animals from being worked to death. Because even the poorest among us need time off to honor God and their physical bodies. Because the land needs to lie fallow so it can replenish itself. Why don't we murder? Because every person is made in the image of God.

But all we have to do is look around at the world to know we never outgrow the need for these basic rules. John Wesley points out that Christians don't own this kind of ethics. "Heathen honesty," he calls it. When Jesus told a story about a man wounded on the side of the road, he made a Samaritan the hero of his story, to remind his listeners that God's chosen people didn't have a monopoly on decency. We don't ignore people in need because that's one of our basic rules. It implies a general responsibility toward the rest of society. Exodus 21:33 says that we shouldn't dig a pit and leave it uncovered, in case an animal falls into it. If we're going to live together and experience God's grace through one another, we can't be negligent of other living beings in our community.

These rules extend beyond personal conduct and touch on social evils, also. "Doom to those who pronounce wicked decrees, and keep writing harmful laws to deprive the needy of their rights," says Isaiah 10:1-2. Bribes, slander, and injustice tarnish not only our souls, but all of society.

Wesley made "do no harm" the first of the General Rules of Methodist Societies. In "The Almost Christian," he says this is part of "having the form of godliness." By itself, it's not enough. But it's the place we all begin. During Advent, the beginning of the Christian year, it's appropriate for us to return to this as a foundation of the Christian life.

We all start our life and our spiritual journey as toddlers. We long to be grown-ups, but our immaturity causes us to wound ourselves, wound one another, and wound God's good creation. But God, like a loving parent, gives us a set of simple norms. Like children, we learn to live together according to a basic level of human decency. If the world could even live up to this standard, we would be closer to the reign of God.

*Rev. Dave Barnhart*

# Do I do good with all my might?

Preparing for Christmas can seem like it's all about quantity—do we have enough gifts for everyone on our list? Do we have enough food for our family's big meal, and that classroom party, and the cookie exchange? Do we have enough time to fit everything in? And enough money to pay for it all? I remember at the first church I served, whenever we had a potluck meal—or, as we call them in the South, "covered-dish dinners"—the kitchen crew was always worried before we served. Will we have *enough* food? (Spoiler alert: we always had *more* than enough!) We feel this in all areas of our lives. In our work: are we doing enough, earning enough? With our families: are we spending enough quality time? In school: did I study enough? Or in general: do I take good enough care of myself?

John Wesley's question, at first, can seem like another one to add to this list: do I do *enough* good in the world? That's a scary question. How much will ever really be enough, and enough for whom—for yourself? for the world? for God? For one thing, we could exhaust ourselves doing good, and we know it still wouldn't be enough for a world full of hurts and needs. For another thing, we know that God is not sitting somewhere with a legal pad, keeping a tally of our good deeds, waiting for us to get to some certain number. I just know God has bigger fish to fry.

But what if, instead of being about quantity, this question was about *quality*? Wesley's question recalls a verse from Ecclesiastes: "Whatever your hand finds to do, do it with all your might" (9:10 NIV). It doesn't mean "try to do everything you possibly can." It means "whatever you choose to do, whatever you are called to do, do it with all your might." Do it with all your power, all your strength. Put your whole self into it. A wise older gentleman once told me, "If a task is first begun, never leave it till it's done. Be ye great or be ye small, do it well or not at all."

These days we have so many things competing for our time, our money, and our attention. We do not need to try to take on everything. As a matter of fact, we may need to take on less. We do not need more *quantity* in our lives. But we can judiciously choose what to put our hands to, and once we choose those things, we can do them with all the good that is in our power. I once was in charge of training mentors to work with children at our local elementary school. In doing my research, I learned that studies have shown that mentors who work with a child for less than a year can actually do more harm than good. Most children need adults they can count on, long-term. We may be able to mentor only one child, or take on only one project, or do one good deed today. But we can do those things with all of our might. Let that be our focus this Advent. We can give that child our fullest attention, our best knock-knock jokes, and a snack (because we know everything is better with a snack). We cannot just hand someone on the street a dollar—we could ask him his name, or how he's doing today. We can do things with a *quality* that truly shows that God's kingdom is breaking into our world again and again. What better witness to our longing for Christ?

*Rev. Monica Beacham*

## 6

# Do I seriously follow God's commandments whenever I can?

I wonder what difference police officers experience on the road as drivers. During work hours, they drive about in vehicles that are clearly identifiable as police cars. But during off-hours, they drive about in cars that blend right in with the rest of ours. And I wonder how different those two experiences are.

My guess is that when an officer drives an ordinary car, he or she sees a lot of ordinary driving. People exceed the speed limit, they signal less, they hurry through yellow lights, and they observe some stop signs rather casually. On the other hand, when an officer drives in a recognizable police car, I expect they find themselves surrounded by exemplary drivers.

The sight of a police car inspires a real carefulness in most of us. We become commendably attentive to everything we're doing and to all the rules of the road. We set our phones aside, put both hands on the wheel, and remember all the good habits we were taught when we first learned how to drive.

The look of such careful driving brings Moses to mind. When Moses said his farewell to the children of Israel, he impressed upon them all of the benefits that come with living God's way. It is a magnificent litany, as we read how the blessings of God will touch every area of life and permeate every aspect of the people's existence. Yet all of it is contingent upon one condition. At the very beginning of the chapter, Moses tells the people, "Now it shall be, if you diligently obey the LORD your God, being careful to do all His commandments which I command you today, the LORD your God will . . ." (Deuteronomy 28:1 NASB). Then come the promises and the blessings.

"Diligently obey." "Careful to do." We know what that looks like when the police car is near. Likewise, we know what carefulness is when handling something that is brand-new, fragile, or expensive. And we know what diligence is when managing an important responsibility. Such carefulness and diligence, Moses would tell us, is meant to be the look of how we treat the commandments of God.

On the other hand, we also know what it looks like to be casual, to cut corners, to play fast and loose. The things we handle carefully are preserved. The things that we handle carelessly, on the other hand, are often broken, including the laws of God.

Thus we are challenged by the question from Mr. Wesley: "Do I seriously follow God's commandments whenever I can?"

It's a self-diagnostic question, and so we will have to be honest with ourselves in order to answer it properly. But we should know the answer because we know the difference between what it looks like to be careful and to be careless. We are familiar with the diligence of drivers when the police officer is near. And so we should be able to discern in ourselves the degree to which we are handling the law of God with the seriousness and care it deserves.

Our experience as Christians, of course, differs from the experience of drivers in two important respects.

First, we observe that the way people drive changes when a police officer is nearby, but how we live out the commandments of God does not feature that sort of variation. We live, after all, with a constant sense of God's nearness. During this season of the year, we celebrate the coming of Emmanuel—God with us—and so we obey carefully at all times because we know we are in God's presence at all times.

And, second, most folks' compliance to traffic laws is motivated by self-interest. We don't want either the expense or the danger of breaking the law. But our careful obedience of God is of a higher sort. "If you love Me," Jesus said, "you will keep My commandments" (John 14:15 NASB). Just as his coming to us was motivated by love, so, too, our obedience to him is motivated by love. We will follow well the commandments of God when they are not about tickets or accidents, but about love.

*Rev. David Kalas*

## *Hymn Reflection*:
## "Come Thou Long-Expected Jesus"

This hymn was first published by Charles Wesley in 1744 in a collection of hymns celebrating the birth of Christ. The two simple verses contain some powerful petitions and repetitions. Dr. Michael Hawn, professor of sacred music at Perkins School of Theology, invites us to pay attention to the six imperative verbs:

*Come . . . release . . . find . . . bring . . . rule . . . raise.*[1] These words have a pleading, almost desperate feel about them. They are meant to capture the deep longing of Israel awaiting the promised Messiah. They are also meant to capture our own longing for a Savior to release us from sin, help us find rest, bring us hope, rule in our hearts, and raise us to God.

Note, too, the repetitions. *Born* is mentioned four times: "born to set thy people free . . . Born thy people to deliver, born a child and yet a King, born to reign in us forever." We long for the joy of new life. Yet the hope of God doing a new thing in us comes through pleading. To say, "Praise be to God!" is most meaningful when it follows the plaintiff cry, "How long, O Lord?" Waiting is a necessary discipline for the altogether Christian.

Zechariah the priest models this spiritual attitude. He and his wife, Elizabeth, spent their life together waiting for a baby. By the time they are introduced to us they are well beyond child-bearing years. Despite being devout, they were not able to carry out their covenant responsibility of bearing children. Added to this disappointment was the social stigma, which typically fell on the wife, of God's judgment causing their barrenness. No doubt words like *release us*, *deliver us*, and *be born in us* were repeated petitions in their prayers.

Then, one day, while his division was serving at the temple, Zechariah's name was chosen for the twice-daily ritual of entering the holy place to burn incense. This was a rare opportunity. The Jewish priests at that time were divided into twenty-four divisions. Each division served two weeks a year, and each day two priests were chosen for the honor of burning incense. With a large number of priests and so few opportunities each year, many were never chosen. Once a priest was selected, his name was removed from the list, so each priest would serve once in his life, if at all. On this day Zechariah not only had a once-in-a-lifetime experience, he heard from the angel Gabriel that his prayer had been heard and he and Elizabeth would have a child. That child would be John the Baptist, the forerunner of Jesus.

Waiting precipitated fulfillment. I don't know why God doesn't answer prayers more quickly. Waiting feels like a fruitless nuisance to me most of the time. Yet the Bible affirms that the most significant of saints had to wait before experiencing what they were waiting for. Accepting the importance of waiting, I find that it helps me keep perspective. God is God and I am not. If my prayers were answered on my schedule, God would be little more to me than a magic genie.

As well, I learn to trust God more. Looking with hindsight, I often realize how getting what I want when I wanted it would not have turned out so well. I keep that in mind when I wait and pray for God to help me trust that God's will is prevailing even when I can't see it. As an old saying goes, "What happens in us while we wait is just as important as what we are waiting for."

So what are you waiting for this Advent season? More important, how are you waiting for it?

*Rev. Rob Fuquay*

---

1 Michael Hawn, "History of Hymns: Hymn Expresses Longing for Arrival of Our Savior," Discipleship Ministries of The United Methodist Church, accessed July 17, 2019, https://www.umcdiscipleship.org/resources/history-of-hymns-hymn-expresses-longing-for-arrival-of-our-savior.

---

8

---

# Do I do everything with a sincere plan and desire to please God in every way?

It is easy to get off track in the days of Advent. People often vacillate between two extremes. On one side is the harried holiday event planner, who is hoping a frenetic schedule and fanatical attention to detail will make it a magical time of the year for family and friends. This person is running at full speed with a to-do list in one hand and a credit card in the other, hoping to get everything just right. On the other end of the spectrum is the passive cynic, who avoids cultural rituals whose meaning has grown anemic and festivities that leave him or her weary rather than joyful. This person stays as disconnected as possible, attends to necessities only at the last minute, and hopes for a cold bad enough to offer an excused absence.

John Wesley's question guides us on a path that makes Advent a sacred time of the year and brings us to a centered space where we can uniquely experience the joy of the Lord in the days before Christmas. Wesley asks us to focus our attention on a "plan and desire to please God." Imagine creating a plan whose sole intention is to bring joy to the heart of God. What person would you attend to as a result? What good deed would be done? What group of people would be blessed? What act of generosity would claim your attention as a result?

I recall a day when I felt God tell me to go visit an elderly relative. She was experiencing memory issues and a good deal of confusion, and I feared the trip was unlikely to produce a meaningful visit. I had a lot to do and almost allowed my tasks to outvote the prodding that I experienced as the Holy Spirit encouraged me to make the journey. When I arrived, she smiled and greeted me warmly. We talked of fond memories. I thanked her for the ways she had blessed my life since I was a child. That day she was bright and her mind sharp, and she seemed glad that I had made the trip and come unexpectedly. Driving home, I recall how joyful I felt. It was not the thought that I had blessed my family member. It was the way she blessed me. I considered how I would have felt about the visit if she would have been less lucid and decided that it was simply good to follow God's lead in my plans for the day. I felt the smile of God that we had shared that time, and that I had been able to offer my appreciation of her life and goodness to me. The desire to please God required me to make a plan to do what the Spirit was asking of me. We find such moments of joy and meaning when we make our desire to please God our highest priority.

By asking us to contemplate our "desire to please God in every way," Wesley asks us to consider not only what we do, but the attitude we carry as we do it. When we think of the disposition we are to carry as Christ followers led by the Holy Spirit, the observation of Paul is helpful. Paul tells the Galatians that there is a real contrast to the behaviors and attitudes that once characterized their lives before they knew Christ. At that time, they were driven by whatever mood or disposition occurred to them on any given day. They were self-centered and unpredictable. By contrast, Paul says, "the fruit of the

Spirit is love, joy, peace, patience, kindness, goodness, faithfulness, gentleness, and self-control" (Galatians 5:22-23).

It's time to make your plan to please God every day during Advent. Consider what your plan might be, and pray for God's help to carry it out in the generous spirit of the Christ whose arrival we anticipate.

*Rev. Tom Berlin*

## 9

# Am I, at the very least, observing the qualities of an "almost" Christian?

"Dear God, please forgive me for not studying until tonight. I know it is midnight, and my exam is at 8 a.m. I also realize that I have no good excuses for not opening my book until now. But at least I'm studying now. So, help me remember all these equations tomorrow. Amen."

Whether your prayer was about work, school, or another part of life, many of us have prayed this type of prayer before. I call it the "79.5 Prayer." It is the prayer one prays when one just wants to scrape by with the lowest possible performance that still achieves a "B" grade. After all, the textbook was bought, *some* studying (albeit last minute) was accomplished, and a little effort was made; therefore, God (or the teacher) should pour out abundant grace and just give us the B. Give us the lowest grade that gets us some respectability. A 79.5 percent rounds up to an 80, which gets us our B.

Minimum effort exerted, maximum grace expected.

And since we know that our God is a God of abundant grace, some of us Christians have adopted this mind-set as we journey together in faith. We try to figure out the least we have to do to be considered a Christian. We wonder if we have to participate in corporate worship when the weather is bad outside, or will God understand if we skip because we attended last Sunday? Should I give sacrificially to help those who are in need, or can I just give a little, so that I have enough for my own desires? Must I share my gift of teaching with the children in my church every Sunday, or can't I just help with vacation Bible school for one week instead? Maybe we make up for it by cramming during Advent and Christmas—giving a bit extra, serving a bit more, attending worship more consistently and even one extra time on Christmas Eve.

A lot of Christians are content with a 79.5 kind of discipleship. This 79.5 discipleship is content with following the letter of God's law without the joy of the fullness of God's Spirit. This 79.5 discipleship has forgotten the joy of a relationship with God and God's people. This 79.5 discipleship rationalizes behaviors with phrases like the following:

Well, at least I don't sin like . . .

Those others never lift a finger; I do more than . . .

I remember when I used to help with . . .

Those new people have more energy, I'll let them sign up for . . .

I know they say that there is a need, but I already gave to help with the . . .

But remember that time that I . . .

Why do we Christians strive for a 79.5 in our Christian walks? Why is Christmas often used as a time to cram instead of celebrate Christ's coming with the fullness of joy and longing?

Perhaps we are just tired of worshiping and glorifying God, forgetting that God is deserving of our very best? Maybe we have become detached from God in our spiritual lives, allowing other habits to pull us away from prayer, study, service, and other means of God's grace.

Whatever the reasoning for our condition, it behooves all of us as flawed, fallen Christians to examine our hearts for the contagious symptoms of complacency and contentment. Wesley's question reminds us that the outward, "almost Christian" life is necessary but not sufficient. If we strive for 79.5 discipleship, we won't even get that far.

Instead, we can strive for wholehearted faith and love of God, with joy that we get to be a part of God's kingdom-building work! After all, we all believe the words Jesus tells his followers in John 10:10, "I came so that they could have life—indeed, so that they could live life to the fullest."

That fullness of life is a gift of grace to us now. It demands that we give *all* of ourselves in joyful surrender to our God. May we see God not as a 79.5 percent burden, but as a 100 percent joy.

*Rev. Robin C. Wilson*

# Am I willing to go a step further and be an "altogether" Christian?

Are you ready for the Christmas rush? In order to stay a step ahead, I find myself becoming more dependent on my to-do list. I write down lists of possible gifts to buy for people. I write down ideas for Christmas worship. I make a list of community events and church parties I want to attend. I add to my to-do list everything I think needs to get done for a good Christmas.

I focus on my to-do list to guide my days. I believe that if I get the list done, then I'll be altogether prepared for Christmas. But the list is never completed, and I often end each day with a longer list than when I started. My hope for a good Christmas begins to fade as I struggle with the weight of everything that remains undone. I find myself choosing to work more hours, rushing from here to there, and trying to pick up the pace as I feel like I am falling behind.

Then I hear the words of James:

*Be patient, therefore, beloved, until the coming of the Lord. The farmer waits for the precious crop from the earth, being patient with it until it receives the early and the late rains. You also must be patient. Strengthen your hearts, for the coming of the Lord is near.*
*(James 5:7-8 NRSV)*

"Be patient," James instructs his fellow Christians. These words are remarkable since, earlier in the letter, James offers one of the most famous Bible passages: "Faith without works is dead" (2:26 KJV). James seems like he could be the patron saint of the to-do list, but James is not telling us to keep ourselves busy. James calls us to an active faith that includes practicing patience.

We often think of patience as passive inaction. James's word of patience is not "just let go and let God," but a call to active expectation of God's new thing about to burst forth! James offers a parable of a farmer who patiently waits for both the early and late rains to produce a precious crop. This beautiful image of rain reminds us of God's work of pouring out from the heavens and fulfilling God's promise on earth. Our active patience gives us time to pay attention to how God is at work in the world around us, and to discern what we can do to cooperate with God. Patience reminds us that the center of our faith isn't our own abilities or accomplishments; our full faith is found in Jesus Christ who accomplishes on our behalf more than we could ever ask or expect.

While I can't completely give up my Christmas to-do list, I can change how I use it. I can prayerfully review the items each day to discern where God is guiding me. I can remove some items to create more space for what Jesus is doing in my life. I will let my faith in Christ guide my day. I will take a patient step toward an altogether, God-filled Christmas.

*Rev. Todd Salmi*

## 11

# Is the love of God shed abroad in my heart?

I had a chance to sit in my four-year-old son's school chapel service. During the welcome, his teacher asked the class full of jumpy children to "name one thing that you did today that you didn't think was possible." Feeling unsure of what my response would be, I was shocked by how quickly every single one of Freddy's classmates thrust their hands into the air. Each one of them was so excited to respond. They all had something to say!

Has anybody asked you this question before? How did you answer?

The apostle Paul encouraged the earliest church to accomplish the impossible when he said, "Glory to God, who is able to do far beyond all that we could ask or imagine by his power at work within us" (Ephesians 3:20). Jesus encouraged his disciples to do the same thing when he said, "I assure you that whoever believes in me will do the works that I do. They will do even greater works than these because I am going to the Father" (John 14:12).

Christ's followers should strive to be people who do things that are considered beyond the realm of possibility.

John Wesley asked, "Is the love of God shed abroad in my heart?" This is a question of impossibility, that the love of God would reside in our heart, and yet we know that the impossible is God's specialty. What else is the Incarnation, the birth of Jesus we celebrate at Christmas, than the impossible event of God becoming human?

God is anything but predictable. God is always surprising. He comes to us as a baby, offers us life in death, says that in giving we receive, the first are last, the lost are found. God has a propensity for the unexpected and longs for us to see this. Time and time again, Jesus assures us that we have the power to do the things that God does. Paul tells the early church that we can accomplish the unimaginable. Our life together as followers of Christ is rooted in believing this. To live a life of faith is to live a life that seeks to love others in ways that are beyond possible, in the same surprising way that Jesus first loved us.

We are to live like Christ, who entered our world humbly as a child born in a manger, whose arrival was announced first to shepherds watching their flocks instead of to princes and rulers.

Live like Christ, who engaged people, all people, no matter who they were, saying, "I love you and there's nothing you can do about it."

Live like Christ, who invited people to experience his love by saying, "Follow me." Christ didn't say believe in me, trust in me, understand me, or defend me. He simply invited people, saying, "Follow me," and they did, all kinds of people—fishermen, tax collectors, sinners, people of great faith, and people who had no faith at all.

If Jesus was anything, he was the kind of person who made everybody a little uncomfortable, because he absolutely loved everybody all the time, but especially those who were deemed unlovable.

The church is the living body of Christ. It is a group of people who live and love like Jesus, who don't conform to the world, but are transformed by a love and unwavering devotion to the good news of Jesus Christ. It's an eclectic community of people who compel others by their actions and who invite others with their words to come and see a love that is dumbfounding and contagious and makes us better.

Does your life reflect the genuine love-filled action of Christ—the humble, sacrificial, unconditional, surprising love of God?

The one born in the manger invites us to let our lights so shine before others. He calls us to live lives of surprising visibility. He commands us to go out and be seen. Are you answering his call?

*Rev. Scott Chrostek*

# Can I cry out, "My God, and my All"?

A transformative moment in my life occurred when I was a college student. A pastor of the church I was attending asked a simple question in his sermon: "Are you fully devoted to God?" I don't know why the question hit me so profoundly that day. I'd been a Christian and had been active in my church as a youth, and I was a weekly participant in campus ministry activities. I read my Bible daily. I was doing all the things I had been told to do in order to cultivate a vibrant Christian life, but this question of full devotion to God caused me to do a gut check. Was I fully devoted; was I all in? I finally acknowledged that I may have been running at high percentages of devotion, but wasn't all the way there. Was I OK with being a 60 percent or 70 percent Christian? Could I honestly cry out, as Wesley puts it, "My God, and my All"?

Advent gives us an opportunity to ask that question of ourselves and to commit to being a wholehearted follower of Christ. When we begin to do this, our lives change. Though the phrase belongs to a different liturgical season, Jesus' words at Gethsemane resonate with this theme when he says, "Not my will, but yours be done" (Luke 22:42 NRSV). Think about the Lord's Prayer when we pray, "your kingdom come, your will be done" (Matthew 6:10 NIV). It just so happens that most of us are really good at making sure that *our* will is done. How does that old Sinatra song go? "I did it my way." Yes, we are good at singing such songs. But in Colossians 3, Paul teaches us that our lives are "hidden with Christ in God" and that Christ is our life (3:3-4). Paul is exhorting us in Colossians 3 to give our all to Christ and make Christ our all in all. Paul says:

> *Therefore, as God's choice, holy and loved, put on compassion, kindness, humility, gentleness, and patience. Be tolerant with each other and, if someone has a complaint against anyone, forgive each other. As the Lord forgave you, so also forgive each other. And over all these things put on love, which is the perfect bond of unity. The peace of Christ must control your hearts—a peace into which you were called in one body. And be thankful people.*
>
> *(Colossians 3:12-15)*

Perhaps there are other questions that we could ask to discern whether we've made God our all in all. God, have I given you every part of my life at school or at work? Have I given you every part of my relationships with family and friends? Have I fully made God a part of my relationship with my spouse or significant other? What about kids? Have I made God my all in all in the ways that I parent my children? Have I given God every part of my financial life and my life of service? These are but a few of the questions that we can ask ourselves to help us answer the larger question of whether God has become our all in all or if God still only has parts and pieces of our lives. As we approach Christmas, my hope for you is that you both acknowledge and grow deeply in your need for God each and every day.

*Rev. Justin Coleman*

## 13

# Do I desire nothing but God?

I've got two mirrors in my bathroom that sit at 90-degree angles with each other. When you look at yourself in my bathroom mirror, there is not much that remains hidden. The many angles ensure that you get an eyeful of yourself. For good or for bad, you see the truth.

John Wesley's question "Do I desire nothing but God?" serves as our spiritual mirror, reflecting the hard truths of our spiritual condition. As I read Wesley's sermon "The Almost Christian," this question convicts me: Is God my daily desire? Hmm.

John Wesley asked tough questions of his listeners, questions that few of us could answer affirmatively with 100 percent confidence. Yet I see his questions as aspirations rather than condemnations. Of course we struggle with answering these questions. That's the point! To grow in Christ means to be stretched in the areas of our lives these questions touch upon. The Christian life entails moving from one point of faith to another.

So, if these questions are aspirational, then I can be honest with where I am now in relation to them and compare that to where I've been.

"Do I desire nothing but God?" Maybe on my best days I come close to answering yes to this question. Yet for most days I'm far from it. Most days I'm hoping to get through the day, make progress at work, spend time with my wife and kids, and find some personal meaning in the process. Is God a part of my day? Absolutely. But the reflection from this question highlights to me that while God is part of my daily life, God often doesn't represent my chief desire. That's most days.

Yet at Christmastime, things shift. I love the Advent season because it's a time of acute awareness of the coming Christ. January through November has its own spiritual rhythm, but December has another. Like with the anticipation of the birth of my own child, there is a gleeful anticipation as I wait for the Christmas remembrance that God has come to dwell among us. Who doesn't want the hope and redemption that the birth of this Christ Child brings? With all the pomp and circumstance that surround Christmas, how can we not turn our desires to the God who desired us above all else?

> *God chose us in Christ to be holy and blameless in God's presence before the creation of the world. God destined us to be his adopted children through Jesus Christ because of his love.*
>
> *(Ephesians 1:4-5)*

Before the universe came into being, God desired to be with you. At Christmas we celebrate the birth of Jesus who came to solidify that relationship between us and the Divine. At Christmas I am reminded of how much I need a Savior to connect with me and to save me. At Christmas I recognize I can't do it all on my own. At Christmas, I long for Jesus.

What about you? This Christmas do you desire nothing but God? Let Wesley's question reveal the truth, whatever that may be. If the answer is yes, then how do you keep that desire for God into the new year? If the answer is no, that's OK. You can't grow in your relationship with Christ if you aren't honest about where you are right now. From now until Christmas, pray this prayer: "God, give me a heart for you." Pray that prayer every time you see evidence of Christmas around you, and I believe that you'll see your desire for Christ's presence in your life change for the better.

"Do I desire nothing but God?" May this Christmas the answer be "Yes! Thanks be to God, yes!"

*Rev. David Dorn*

---

14

---

## *Hymn Reflection*:
## "Peace upon earth be restored"

What could possibly be a bigger dream, wish, hope, and prayer than for "peace upon earth be restored"? It feels impossible, almost ridiculous. Peace on earth? Nations war with nations. Politicians seem to be in a constant state of discord. Communities are filled with hate and prejudice. Churches divide over doctrine. Even in our own families, we struggle to get along with one another. In fact, when I pray these words, as much as I long for peace on earth, I admit it's hard to believe the day will ever come. And yet when I read the words of this hymn, I find Charles Wesley offering assurance that Jesus has already come to restore peace: "O Jesus, exalted on high, . . . [who] Didst stoop to redeem a lost race: / Once more to thy creatures return, / And reign in thy kingdom of grace."[1]

In practical terms, what is Wesley talking about? As you continue reading his lyrics, you are seized by his conviction that, when Christ appeared in the flesh, the world became united with the Prince of Peace: "No horrid [alarm] of war . . . No sound of the trumpet is there / Where Jesus' spirit o'erflows."

Perhaps Wesley is suggesting that peace isn't a faraway dream, and in fact, that we can experience it every day. Rather than waiting for the world to be peaceful, we have a more active task of embracing the quiet and peaceable reign of Jesus in our own hearts. When we turn over our angers, disappointments, and frustrations to God, then God is there to give us peace. This is the peace that surpasses our understanding (Philippians 4:7), a peace that actually might begin to change the world one person at a time.

This lesson hit home to me years ago when a dear friend told me about her work as a weekend counselor at a Christian retreat center. I somewhat naively asked her how she could possibly help someone in need in only one weekend. She had a ready answer: "Because every problem, every hurt, every broken relationship ultimately requires the same spiritual discipline." Well, I had to hear this one! "What is it?" I asked. She replied with total confidence: "Let go and let God. As simple as it sounds, that is what is needed. That is when the peace comes."

At first I had to stifle a laugh. Of course I'd heard that expression all my life. But her seriousness told me she embraced this familiar mantra as a moment-to-moment practice. It has since become my practice, as well. When I surrender to God, I'm not giving up on the battles and challenges in my daily life. Instead, I am embracing the truth that God is in control. When I do, my situation may not change, but I change internally. I find what I am seeking the most: peace.

During this Advent season, I pray that we lay down our swords, both our external weapons of words and deeds that hurt others and our internal weapons of resentments, anger, hatred, and prejudices. And then I pray that we trust God. Surely this is the path to peace for all the Earth.

*Susan Fuquay*

---

1 Charles Wesley, "All Glory to God in the Sky," Hymnary.org, accessed July 16, 2019, https://hymnary.org/text/all_glory_to_god_in_the_sky.

## 15

# Am I happy in God?

When I read this question the first thing that comes to my mind is, "What's the alternative?" If we do not find our happiness in God, where do we find it? I think the usual answer is that we look for happiness in the circumstances of our life. I know that I do.

Most of us understand happiness as an emotion or a feeling that is dependent on how life is at any particular moment. We can be happy one day and not so happy another. It all depends on how things are going. Think about it. Most of us correlate happiness with things going well in life. Happiness is a product of enjoying your job, being in a good place with relationships, not being overly stressed, having some amount of financial stability, or being in good health. When life is generally going well, we are happy. In other words, happiness is dependent on the circumstances of our life. This seems to make sense. But it also reveals a problem. If happiness is dependent on the circumstances of life, then it is an unstable feeling. As soon as we experience challenge, disappointment, tragedy, or hardship, we no longer are happy. We find that happiness is fleeting.

But Scripture talks about a different kind of happiness, one that isn't dependent on the circumstances of our life. In his Letter to the Philippians, Paul writes, "Be glad in the Lord always! Again I say, be glad!" (4:4).

How in the world are we supposed to be glad *always*? Rejoice *always*? Be happy *all the time*? Is Paul just being unrealistic here, or naive? No, neither of these. In fact, if you dig in a little, what you find is that Paul actually wrote this letter during a low point in his life. Imprisoned and awaiting trial, Paul wrote this letter during a time of significant suffering and personal challenge. Paul was not unfamiliar with hardship, and he certainly wasn't asking us to pretend like everything is OK even when it is not.

Instead, Paul is encouraging us to shift our understanding of happiness, to change what we base our happiness on, or what we put our hope in. When we put our hope in the circumstances of our life, we will endlessly be trying to control and stabilize the forces of our life in a futile pursuit to "find happiness." It usually doesn't work, and even if we happen to find that perfect balance where everything in our life is working out, it doesn't last long. Jobs are lost, relationships go through turmoil, illness hits, and the unexpected befalls us. Putting our hope for happiness in circumstances is a recipe for never finding it and being frustrated in the process.

Instead, Paul encourages us to put our hope for happiness not in circumstances of our life but in the power of God. This kind of happiness (often distinguished as joy) is found in something deeper, more significant, more stable, and indeed eternal. This is the kind of happiness that cannot be taken away by a bad day or ruined by life's challenges. This is the kind of happiness that allows us to be sad, to feel disappointment, to get angry, and to suffer life's inevitable hardships still knowing that God has not abandoned or left us. This is a joy that comes not in everything going well all the time, but in the deep belief that God will walk through every dark period with us and will see us through to the other side. This is a happiness that cannot be shaken or taken away, because God is not shaken, and

God's work to bring about good in our lives cannot be thwarted. As the Resurrection shows us, even death itself cannot defeat us or define our future.

This Christmas season, ask yourself, "Where am I looking for happiness?" Is your happiness dependent on the perfect Christmas dinner or family members all getting along? Is it rooted in a certain feeling that you hope to give or a certain gift you hope to receive? Is it based on details working out just the way you want and your expectations of others being met? If it is, then Christmas is bound to disappoint. But instead, this Christmas I invite you to remember that our happiness and joy don't come from life's circumstances, which will be great one day and not so great another. Rather, our circumstances come from a God who is coming to dwell with us, to walk beside us, to never leave us, and to work for the ultimate good in our lives and in the life of the world.

*Rev. Matt Miofsky*

## 16

# Is God my glory, my delight, and my source of joy?

Watch for it along the way to Christmas. It may take you by surprise. It's easily missed amid the delightful chaos and beautiful clutter of the season. It's the joy of anticipation. It's the joy we experience when we find the perfect gifts for people we love, and anticipate the look of surprise on their faces when they open them on Christmas morning. It's the joy of sending Christmas cards and imagining the way people will feel when they receive them. It's the joy we feel in anticipation of a greater joy to come; the joy of hoping for a gift we have yet to receive. Biblically, it's the joy of anticipating that joy-soaked day when God's kingdom comes and God's will is fully done on earth as it became flesh in Jesus and is already fulfilled in heaven.

I think that's what John Wesley had in mind when he said that being "altogether Christians" includes "rejoicing in hope of the glory of God." He borrowed that phrase from Paul, who commands us to "rejoice in hope" (Romans 12:12 NRSV). We are encouraged to experience joy not merely in the memory of "Christmas Past," but in our assurance of "Christmas Yet to Come."

When C. S. Lewis told the story of his journey from arid agnosticism into vibrant faith, he described it as his longing for and experience of Joy, a word he consistently capitalized. He called Joy "an unsatisfied desire which is itself more desirable than any other satisfaction." He said that the one and only characteristic that Joy has in common with happiness or pleasure is that "anyone who has experienced it will want it again."[1] The difference is that happiness and pleasure often depend on our circumstances and are largely within our power to create or control, but Joy is always an undeserved gift from God. That's why he titled his spiritual autobiography *Surprised by Joy*.

Paul's command to "rejoice in hope" is set in the context of his description of specific behaviors that shape our lives around the hope we share. This joy is not simply an internal emotion. It is joy that becomes flesh in the way we live. It enables us to live now in ways that are consistent with the future for which we hope. It is the joy we saw in Archbishop Desmond Tutu. During the darkest days of the struggle against apartheid, his courageous leadership was consistently infused with irrepressible joy in the assurance that God's promise of freedom would one day be fulfilled. It was the joy of anticipation of what was yet to come.

Dietrich Bonhoeffer described the same joy in his last letter to his former students before he was imprisoned. He fearlessly named the suffering they were facing, but he affirmed that "joy abides with God, and it comes down from God and embraces spirit, soul, and body; and where this joy has seized a person, there it spreads, there it carries one away, there it bursts open closed doors."[2]

Watch for joy along the way to Christmas and along the journey from being "almost" to "altogether" Christian. It may come when you least expect it. It's the joy that rejoices in the hope of what is yet to come.

*Rev. James A. Harnish*

---

1  C. S. Lewis, *Surprised by Joy* (New York: Harcourt, Brace & World, 1955), 18.

2  Dietrich Bonhoeffer, "The Road to Freedom: Dietrich Bonhoeffer's Last Writings," selected and edited by Susannah Black, Plough.com, accessed July 18, 2019, https://www.plough.com/en/topics/faith/witness/last-writings-of-dietrich -bonhoeffer.

# Is this commandment written in my heart: "That he who loves God loves others also"?

Each of us has our own faith journey and our own experiences and understandings of how we show God that we love God. While our relationship with God may be private, held between you and God, the way we live our lives is a reflection of how we love God and how we aspire to love our neighbors.

In "The Almost Christian," John Wesley lays out the truth that someone can be moral, ethical, and loving without professing a faith. A person who is not a Christian and who is kind, generous, and thoughtful is not necessarily a depraved, immoral heathen. Along the same lines, a Christian who has a surface-level faith—kind, generous, engages in a couple of surface spiritual disciplines—is not an evil person either. But John Wesley's writings encourage the Christian to have depth to his or her faith and to have a deep thread of love toward God, a depth of knowledge and experience of how God loves each of us, and a substantial, meaningful love of others.

Doing the right thing matters. Caring for others and showing love for them are good things. Showing love to others can take a multitude of forms: acts of service, uplifting words, a helping hand. But Wesley reminds us that no matter how we end up showing love to others, our mind-set, our motivations, and our intentions matter. That's why the commandment to love others must be written on the heart. When it comes to loving others, it is good to "do the right thing." But it is best if we engage in loving activities from a heart of love—so that our actions are an expression of the love for others that's written in our hearts.

In this season of your life, do you struggle with loving others? You may find it to be second nature to be polite, gracious, and kind to others. You may even engage in some acts of service around the Advent and Christmas season, like giving to the food pantry, participating in a gift exchange in the office, or hosting a neighborhood party. Are you taking on these actions out of obligation or as a way to genuinely love your neighbor? Are these habits without meaning? Or are they a reflection of how you strive to love and care for others?

We are not called to overextend ourselves in order to demonstrate love for others. But a Wesleyan understanding of love means that when we do engage in acts of love for others, our motivations matter. In this season of caretaking, celebration, worship, and gatherings around the table, consider how you want to show love to others.

Showing love to others doesn't have to be overly complicated. In the Advent and Christmas narratives in the New Testament, love for others was shown in simple ways—Elizabeth opening up her home to Mary, the angel reassuring the terrified shepherds of their safety, Mary whispering truth and love to her newborn child.

Where is God inviting you to show love to others? What acts of love in the New Testament resonate with you? Who is in your day-to-day circle that would be receiving your acts of love? Consider where the Holy Spirit is nudging you to move from simply loving God to loving your neighbor as well.

*Rev. April Casperson*

---

**18**

---

## Do I love my neighbor as myself?

As a preacher's kid, I moved a lot as a child. My family moved every five to six years, it seemed, when a new pastoral appointment sent us to a new church. I came to dread the yearly possibility of a move and held out hope that one day I would never have to move again. My hope was nurtured by family members who would welcome us at holidays and periodic visits, whose homes were sources of stability and constancy amid life's changes.

As I consider Wesley's question in light of this hope of my childhood, I see that my hope was incomplete because it only focused on me. I minister with people on the streets who experience homelessness and have come to recognize that not everyone has family or community to walk alongside them in life's journey or to greet them with love upon arrival. When I realized that I was part of the whole family of Christ, I realized what an altogether hope would require. It would require me to love my neighbor as myself, to hope for their well-being as much as I hoped for my own.

Over two thousand years ago, hope showed up in a baby, the best symbol of hope there is! Hope was laid in a manger—literally a feeding trough—a sign that generations could feed on this hope to keep going. God showed up in the last place anybody would choose to give birth, showing us that no place on earth is beyond hope's reach.

The people I meet on the streets mirror how God showed up then and keeps showing up now. We need to be open to these neighbors of ours who show what hope looks like in different places. Each of us carries a piece that is meant to be shared, and when we love our neighbors as we love ourselves, we find that hope grows stronger together.

This kind of hope travels. When one person gets it, a string of others catch it. At first it came to me through my nuclear family. Then it came through various other relationships along the way. Now it is the beloved community of all those I've come to know and love. And as it moved outward through the love of neighbor, it grew from an almost to an altogether hope—one that envisions the well-being of the whole world.

This Advent, we have an opportunity to experience an altogether hope. I believe such a hope occurs when we hold out hope not only for ourselves, but for our neighbors as well. Wesley's question reminds us that loving our neighbor is at the foundation of the Christian life. May we commit ourselves to loving others and experiencing hope that is grounded in that love.

*Rev. Ingrid McIntyre*

---

**19**

---

Do I love everyone,
even my enemies,
even the enemies of God,
as my own soul?

A few years ago, I was privileged to spend two days with renowned New Testament scholar N. T. Wright. I asked him, "What characterized the first followers of Jesus?" He quickly responded, "It was their passionate love for each other and their care for the poor and diseased." During Advent we light a candle to represent the love that Jesus brings. And it's not a stretch to say that more than anything else, the litmus test for fidelity in following Jesus is the high call to love people. Think about the witnesses of Scripture to this truth. In the Upper Room with his apprentices, Jesus told them straight:

> *"So now I am giving you a new commandment: Love each other. Just as I have loved you, you should love each other. Your love for one another will prove to the world that you are my disciples."*
> *(John 13:34-35 NLT)*

From foot washing as an example in John 13 to the "fruit that lasts" in John 15, the rubber meets the road for Jesus in our willingness to love people. The author of 1 John wrote in a similar vein decades later, with these challenging words: "This is the message you have heard from the beginning: We should love one another" (3:11 NLT).

Similarly the author of 1 Peter emphasized love in our relationships with others:

*Finally, all of you should be of one mind. Sympathize with each other. Love each other as brothers and sisters. Be tenderhearted, and keep a humble attitude. Don't repay evil for evil. Don't retaliate with insults when people insult you. Instead, pay them back with a blessing. That is what God has called you to do, and he will grant you his blessing.*

*(1 Peter 3:8-9 NLT)*

Jesus even had the audacity in the Sermon on the Mount to up the ante regarding love. He teaches:

*"You have heard the law that says, 'Love your neighbor' and hate your enemy. But I say, love your enemies! Pray for those who persecute you! In that way, you will be acting as true children of your Father in heaven."*

*(Matthew 5:43-45a NLT)*

As a self-described "man of one book," Mr. John Wesley knew this high calling to love for those of us who follow the Rabbi from Nazareth. His searching question, "Do I love everyone, even my enemies, even the enemies of God, as my own soul?" cuts to the quick and reveals the distance yet to be traveled in our pilgrimage with our triune God for all of us. We all fall short in our capacity to love people well. Advent is a time to remember our calling to love all people and to commit ourselves to love as a way of preparing our hearts and lives for Jesus.

The high calling is not the problem, after all. It's the execution of living a life of radical love that is our dilemma. Because let's be honest. People are messy and relationships are hard. I believe the avenue to indeed loving all people regardless of circumstance is acknowledging that you can't. As a person in recovery, I love the Twelve Steps. Step 1 reminds us of our powerlessness:

> *We admitted we were powerless over alcohol—that our lives had become unmanageable.*

In the words of Wesley, loving "everyone, even my enemies, even the enemies of God" requires a power greater than ourselves. It is only as "the love of God is shed abroad in our hearts" (Romans 5:5 KJV) that God's love can splash out of us and onto others. The good news is that this power greater than ourselves is coming into the world. Jesus is coming to us as God with us.

Recently, I spoke with one of the mature saints in our church who was raised in a very proper church where everyone was just like him. Our diverse congregation and ministries have stretched him. He told me with tears in his eyes, "If you had told me that I'd know and love drug addicts, prostitutes, and people with all kinds of tattoos, I'd have told you that you were crazy. But I do." My friend is learning Jesus' way of loving everyone.

*Rev. Jorge Acevedo*

# 20

# Do I love others as Christ loved me?

I spent many years stuck in anxiety, fear, and panic attacks while also serving as a United Methodist pastor. It was eerie to stand up and share a message of love and grace that I fully believed, while also sensing a lion in the room about to pounce. One day, it finally got bad enough that I knew it was time to go deeper into my fear. Once I was ready to do the work, to befriend my fear and hear what it was trying to tell me, God invited me into all kinds of resurrections. A beautiful new life emerged that's grounded in a deeper beauty of God. My identity has always been as a child of God. But taking this intentional step into the hidden parts of my life invited me to an altogether life, not just an almost life.

Today we ask: *Do I love others as Christ loved me?*

There are two parts here. Do I allow Christ to love me? Do I love others? The order of these two questions is crucial.

When we try to love others *before* allowing Christ to love us, we often struggle. When our identities are out of order, it's tough to love others the way Christ loves us. It's tempting to love out of a shallow source of strength. We love out of ego, our own effort, what we think is right, or what we see others do. This is not sustainable. We know it, but we often don't pay attention to this as long as we think it's mostly working. Yet when we allow Christ to love us, we can love others in a way that draws from the strength of this love.

How do we know the love we have for others draws strength from how Christ loves us? That's a great question to reflect on. Sometimes I don't know. At those times I rely on God's grace that works so well in all my areas of pain and brokenness. Other times, I know by the love that bubbles up in my throat for someone that it comes from a place of unbreakable strength. It's so strong that I know it comes from a divine source. Still other times, I trust and believe the love I share with others comes from how Christ loves me. It's a step of faith to love someone I don't understand or don't like.

Our invitation this Advent and all year long is to rightsize our identity in Christ. As we continue our Advent journey, you're invited to make a list of your identities in this season of life. You may be a son, daughter, mother, father, grandparent, child, friend, boss, employee, neighbor, leader, and more. Write down all the identities you hold. Consider putting them in order of their priority in your life. Do you spend more time being a boss than a friend? Is it a season where the parent role is central and the neighbor identity takes a back seat? Be honest. There's no reason to sugarcoat it.

Which identity is at the top of your list? When your primary identity is as a child of God, *then* the act of loving others comes from a place of great depth. That's the lesson I learned when I learned to lean into my anxiety and fear. It doesn't mean it's easy, but it's possible and sustainable in a way our shallow strength can never handle. We burn out when we love from our false selves. We thrive when we love from our identities as children of God.

May you spend hushed moments with the One who made you today, receiving the love God longs to give you. Then may you love one person extravagantly well today!

*Rev. Jenny Smith*

---

**21**

---

*Hymn Reflection*:
"And God Himself is born!"

Sometimes our most precious gifts come in moments when time stands still—moments that create a sacred space—allowing complete surrender to the love that flows from heaven. This was one of those moments.

The glow of flickering candlelight mingled with our voices as we sang in the darkened sanctuary. The atmosphere was rich with reverent anticipation—Christmas was almost here!

A young mother stood in front of me, swaying gently with the rhythm of the music. Her baby boy, whom I guessed to be a couple of months old, lay snuggled against her left shoulder. I marveled at this child's miniature features—his eyes closed in the sweet dreaminess of sleep, his tiny hands gripping long, dark locks of his mother's hair, and his little mouth the shape of a perfect kiss.

As I watched him, I was struck with the thought that not very long ago, this little one's spirit left the very realm we were singing about to begin his life on earth. And then, without warning, the sleeping child opened his eyes, looked at me, and smiled.

In that sparkling moment, time—and my heart—stood still. His eyes held mine as the music wrapped us in a sweet embrace.

There, in that sacred space, I felt as if I was looking upon the face of God.

Music has the wondrous ability to bring us into these blessed moments where we encounter our Creator. Through the inspired writing of Charles Wesley, we find ourselves transported into the very pages and events of the Scriptures. Wesley's Nativity Hymn, "Glory Be to God on High," ushers us into one of Scripture's most sacred events on a quiet, dark night in Bethlehem—to a place bathed in the flickering light of a brilliant star. Here we stand as witnesses with the heavenly host as a King descends from his throne of glory to take his place among us. As the night sky resounds with the praise of angels, a baby boy is placed in a manger.

His tiny hand reaches out for comfort. His precious mouth opens for nourishment. His eyes look upward in search of a mother's love. A tiny miracle has joined the human race: God himself is born!

> *Glory be to God on high,*
> *And peace on earth descend;*
> *Now God comes down, He bows the sky,*
> *And shows Himself our friend!*
> *God the invisible appears,*
> *God the blest, the great I AM,*
> *He sojourns in this vale of tears,*
> *And Jesus is His name.*
>
> *Him by the angels all adored,*
> *Their maker and their king;*
> *Lo, tidings of their humbled Lord*
> *They now to mortals bring;*
> *Emptied of His majesty,*
> *Of His dazzling glories shorn,*
> *Our being's Source begins to be,*
> *And God Himself is born!*[1]

Is it our imagination, or do the stars themselves cry out with joy? Trembling shepherds with sleepy lambs add to our number, and together we approach the lowly stable to meet the blessed Child. In this sacred moment, we fall to our knees in surrender to the love that has arrived from heaven. Are not our hearts already bursting with the desire to belong to him?

The hand that formed the earth and skies reaches out to us in an offer of relationship and peace. The mouth that spoke all of creation into being opens to speak his truth to our hungry hearts and weary souls. The eyes that shine with eternal love look up to seek his image reflected in us.

And then he smiles.

*Jennifer Wilder Morgan*

---

1 Charles Wesley, "Glory Be to God on High," Hymnary.org, accessed July 17, 2019, https://hymnary.org/text/glory_be_to_god_on_high_and_peace_on.

# Do I believe that Christ loved me and gave himself for me?

There are times in our lives when it's difficult to believe, as John Wesley said, that "Christ loved me and gave himself for me." We may wonder, as Mary wondered at the angel's words, "How can this be?" We may feel as if our past is too dark, or we can't possibly be loved by God until we have become more perfect, cleaned up a little better. Otherwise, we are not worthy of such sacrificial love.

A few defining moments in my life have brought assurance that even I am loved by Christ. This is the story of one such moment.

On the first Christmas my husband and I celebrated together as a married couple, the bump barely visible under my winter sweater was a small indicator of the giant-sized joy we were feeling at the recent news that we were going to have a baby. Being pregnant during the Christmas season made me resonate more deeply than ever with Mary's story. This child that we would not meet for months was already loved beyond measure and was, in our minds, a divine miracle offered to us older-aged newlyweds. Like Mary, I felt "favored."

In our unbridled excitement, my husband and I went shopping and bought the kind of gifts we hoped to give to our child one day and deposited them at the local Angel Tree. A bicycle, basketball, dolls, building blocks, and more were offered as reverently as gold, frankincense, and myrrh, because every child, we thought, is worthy of knowing they are a beloved gift from God, especially at Christmas. That Christmas was aglow with joy and hope for the future. All was calm. All was bright.

Fast-forward ten years, and it was a bit less perfect. Two weeks before Christmas, there were precious few gifts under the tree for our now two children, and Christmas cards impatiently waited to be addressed. One morning I wondered, "When will there be time to create the perfect Christmas for my family between work, seminary, and keeping up with two busy children?" By early evening the question didn't matter. I was frantically driving our firstborn to the emergency room where a surgeon and my husband would be waiting to meet us. It was suspected she had a ruptured appendix and time was of the essence. As I glanced to check our limp daughter, moaning in the back seat, I saw our young son's dirty face, clothes, and bare feet. I had hurriedly scooped him up from playing in his sandbox on our way to the car, and only now did I realize he had no shoes. So be it. We weren't turning back.

Darkness was descending as we rounded the corner toward Children's Hospital, and the beautiful blue lights of its towering Christmas tree acted as a beacon directing us toward the emergency room drive. We were almost there. Almost to the lifesaving help our daughter needed. As we pulled up to the drive, our car was abruptly stopped by a sea of traffic barricades and a police officer explaining that we couldn't come through until the tree lighting ceremony, complete with local NFL celebrities and hordes of onlookers, had ended.

My children still tell stories of how, at that moment, my personality turned immediately from the normal pleasant one of the mother they knew into one exhibited by a fiercely aggressive momma bear protecting her cubs. Within seconds we had a police escort into the emergency room! Effusive thanks and apologies followed.

Five days later our daughter was back home, minus an appendix, and recovering in her bed.

The final week before Christmas wasn't spent frantically shopping and addressing Christmas cards. Most days were spent quietly, with our family all piled on the sofa reading Christmas stories together, wrapping the few presents we did have—together—and taking care of the precious gift we had been given ten years before. It is one of our favorite Christmas memories.

It is rare now that I wonder, "How can this be, that Christ loves *me*? That God came in the flesh of a child to give himself up for *me*?" because I know that if the love I have for my own children is so deep, so protective and fierce, how much greater must his love be for me, the precious child he came to save.

Every child of God, including you, should know that there is One who loves you tenderly, fiercely, and aggressively. Even if your past or present is dark. Even if you aren't perfect. Even if you feel dirty or have no shoes.

*Rev. Susan Robb*

# Do I have faith in Christ's blood?

I spent my childhood in a small country church, often listening to my grandmother sing the hymn "Nothing but the Blood" at the top of her lungs with tears in her eyes.

> *What can wash away my sin?*
> *Nothing but the blood of Jesus. . . .*
> *O precious is the flow*
> *that makes me white as snow;*
> *no other fount I know;*
> *nothing but the blood of Jesus.*[1]

"Rachel," she would say, "there's just something about the blood of Jesus. I'm so grateful for his blood!"

Now friends, at first glance you might say that is pretty odd. Why would someone get so emotional about blood? It's especially odd to consider during Advent, when we anticipate Jesus' birth. And I have to be honest, I too have some major reservations when singing about the blood of Jesus. For starters, singing about Jesus' blood kind of makes following Jesus sound like cannibalism or masochism. At the very least it makes us seem like a big group of weirdos. Who sings about blood that flows?

These reservations are real with a growing number of unchurched people walking through the sanctuary doors or worshiping online. Jesus' blood is a foreign and strange concept. If you have no understanding of Jesus' sacrifice on the cross, you may wonder what on earth you've just gotten yourself into when you start singing about Jesus' blood.

And yet, I go back to my grandmother and her tears. My grandmother's tears were real and her gratitude was real. She knew something about the redeeming and restoring nature of Jesus' blood.

She affirmed Paul's declaration in Colossians 1:20, "He reconciled all things to himself through him [Jesus]—whether things on earth or in the heavens. He brought peace through the blood of his cross." My grandma understood that Jesus' blood cleansed her, his blood claimed her. Jesus' blood reconciled her with God and all creation.

My grandma felt the weight of her own stuff—dare I say sin! She knew that Jesus suffered not only for the world, but for her, a fact that overwhelmed her every single time. *What can wash away my sin? Nothing but the blood of Jesus. What can make me whole again? Nothing but the blood of Jesus.*

I do not want to limit Jesus' life, death, and resurrection to the blood he spilled on the cross. The upcoming celebration of Christmas shows us that Jesus' whole life—including his birth, his teachings, his healings—is important. But even during Advent, I continue to embrace the power of the suffering Christ, who lived our life, died our death, and continues to reign with God now and forevermore. As we embrace the suffering of Christ, it readies us to embrace our own suffering as an integral part of our story, God's story. Not that God causes our suffering, but rather we serve a God who suffers with us, who walks with us, and who gives us the strength to work for the liberation of all people. My grandmother experienced the liberation of Jesus, yes even through his blood.

May we be ever grateful for Jesus' blood—blood shed for the redemption, reconciliation, and restoration of the whole world.

*Rev. Rachel Billups*

---

1 Robert Lowry, "Nothing but the Blood," Hymnary.org, accessed July 26, 2019, https://hymnary.org/text/what_can_wash_away_my_sin.

---

**24**

---

## Do I believe that Jesus has taken away my sins and cast them as a stone into the depth of the sea?

Can you affirmatively proclaim, "Yes, I believe!" to Wesley's question?

If you cannot, you have yet to soak in God's radical grace revealed in Jesus.

Until the age of nine, I was in church about every Sunday due to the efforts and faithfulness of my grandparents. They ushered me to Wednesday night children's programming and vacation Bible school. But somehow the God I came to believe in was one who kept a strict ledger of wrongs and rights. It wasn't the God that the church taught, but it is the God I constructed. The "wrongs" side of the ledger began to grow exponentially due to my budding addiction. Broken relationships, self-hatred, and life wreckage followed me like a shadow. Imagining God removing them was unfathomable.

I suspect John Wesley asked this question because for much of his life he couldn't affirm it. He wanted to, but was unable. Condemnation stubbornly hung over him like a thick morning fog. Even though his life was filled with good works and he was an ordained Anglican priest, somehow he was never convinced of

Christ's forgiveness. He knew the Bible. He preached and taught it. Even with the information about Jesus taking his sins away firmly planted into his head, it hadn't fully blossomed in his heart. It wasn't until his profound Aldersgate experience that his whole attitude and outlook were transformed.

Pushing through resistance to go to a small group gathering, John listened to Martin Luther's preface to Romans. He described it this way:

> *While he was describing the change which God works in the heart through faith in Christ, I felt my heart strangely warmed. I felt I did trust in Christ, Christ alone, for salvation; and an assurance was given me that He had taken away my sins, even mine, and saved me from the law of sin and death.* [1]

I don't know why it took Wesley, who had the appearance of a very holy life, so long to experience something in his heart that was so drilled into his head.

Perhaps it is because the claim of the gospel is audacious. Jesus takes away all of our sins. All of them. *Every. Single. One.* Everything you have done; everything that you have failed to do; every unsanctified thought; every attitude or action that has wounded others, yourself, or the world are forgiven and forgotten by the power of Jesus Christ. That's the power that we expect to come to us on Christmas when Christ is born. That's the power that is already at work among us.

Take a moment to reflect upon the most despicable, dishonest, or selfish act you have ever committed. Search your mind for the foulest and most detestable thoughts that have emerged from the dark recesses of your heart. Got them? Whether you've sinned boldly or meekly, Jesus covers them.

Seem preposterous? It is—until it isn't. God's grace penetrates our previously constructed ideas so that we can experience it deep within.

One Aldersgate experience happened to me while listening to a sermon. The preacher used a vivid illustration about forgiveness and a dead armadillo on the side of the road. And although I can't remember the details of the sermon, I knew in that moment that Jesus had forgiven me for everything. And even now, when I see a dead armadillo, I remember that Jesus has taken my sins and cast them as a stone into the depths of the sea.

Wesley couldn't manufacture the moment before it came. Neither could I. And neither will you. But God's grace relentlessly pursues us. God doesn't define us by our worst moments and tendencies, but rather God realigns us through Jesus' life, death, and resurrection. That is the very purpose for which Christ was born. That is what we celebrate tonight.

And while it is an unpleasant exercise to reflect upon one's sins, failures, and brokenness, it reveals something beautiful: the depths of God's love for you and for all of humanity.

Yes, I believe.

How about you?

*Rev. Justin LaRosa*

---

1 John Wesley's journal, May 24, 1738, quoted in Joe Iovino, "Holy Spirit Moments: Learning from Wesley at Aldersgate," May 18, 2017, UMC.org, http://www.umc .org/what-we-believe/holy-spirit-moments-learning-from-wesley-at-aldersgate.

## *Hymn Reflection*:
## "Hark! the Herald Angels Sing"

Christmas Day! I am sure that when you hear these words, memories of the sights, smells, and sounds of family gatherings fill your mind and enrich your soul immediately. For me, the reminder of gathering around the organ at my grandparents' house and singing through the hymnal comes to mind. When we sang, I rarely considered the theological content of what I was singing. But hymns and carols carry an intense amount of theological material. When a hymn writer uses a story from the Bible as the frame for the poem, the story becomes a springboard for deep theological expression, and for the singer, a means of deep theological reflection. The great carol "Hark! the Herald Angels Sing"[1] is an example of a carol that has a strong and well-known story that can propel deep reflection.

The hymn starts with a simple, poetic retelling of the angels' visit to the shepherds as contained in Luke 2:8-14. A careful reader notices that, in fact, the shepherds are never actually mentioned in the song. No, Charles Wesley has the angels address the entire world: "Joyful, all ye nations rise." We are part of that grand earthly sweep confronted by the angels. We are also part of the grand earthly sweep who proclaim, with the angels, "Christ is born in Bethlehem!"

But the second verse starts something quite different—a list of assertions of who this baby is. After reading the carol through, ask yourself these questions:

- What does it mean to recognize Christ as the everlasting Lord?
- What does it mean to accept the idea that Jesus is the offspring of a virgin's womb?
- How can you reconcile the living God, fully divine and yet pleased to dwell in human flesh?
- How do you recognize Christ as the Prince of Peace in your life?
- What does righteousness mean to you, and how do you recognize that righteousness in Jesus?
- Do you fully accept Jesus as your Savior and accept that he brings light and life, and that he is, indeed, risen with healing in his wings?
- Do you believe that Jesus, in his divinity and humanity, was born to free us from death and will raise us to life and give us a second birth?
- Can you freely and loudly sing "Glory to the newborn King!"

I would assume that each of us has a problem answering at least one of these questions. We may have a difficult time even with understanding the question (theologians have fought for years about what "righteousness" means), or with a theological concept (the virgin birth), or even with our own faith (do I believe this enough to freely sing "Glory to the newborn King!").

These questions are very close to the heart of what John Wesley asks in "The Almost Christian." They are aspirational questions that, in Wesley's terms, help point the way to perfection. As we sing of Christ's birth, may these questions propel us to a deeper experience of the love, grace, and salvation he brings.

*Dr. Michael Dougherty*

---

1 "Hark! the Herald Angels Sing," lyrics by Charles Wesley, 1739, is found in *The United Methodist Hymnal* (Nashville, TN: The United Methodist Publishing House, 1989), 240.

---

**26**

---

# Do I believe that Jesus has blotted out the handwriting that was against me, taking it out of the way, nailing it to his cross?

On the TV show *The Good Place*, the moral narrative is that every action in our life has a positive or negative point value. Remember your sister's birthday? Plus 15.02 points! Sexually harass someone? Minus 731.26 points. When you die, all of those actions are tallied up to determine your destination in the afterlife. If you die with a positive score, you get to go to the Good Place. Otherwise you have earned a one-way ticket to the Bad Place.

It got me thinking about how we do the same kind of math in our Christian faith. Only, the calculation has to be adjusted because the baseline for action is not some theoretical neutral, but to fully and completely follow God's ways. "Be perfect, therefore, as your heavenly Father is perfect," Jesus tells us (Matthew 5:48 NRSV). If our aim is to do God's will, then every action that detracts from that ideal is not only a negative, but cannot be restored. As St. Anselm understood it, even if we could make up for the sin, we also must satisfy our offense to God's very honor.

Not living in a medieval society where this ideal of honor makes any sense to us, I sometimes find Anselm's perspective hard to understand. But then I think about how early in my marriage, I wanted to do everything perfectly. But when stress popped up at work, I let everything slip at home. I put the dishes on the counter instead of in the dishwasher. I forgot the laundry in the washing machine overnight and the next day everything smelled moldy. I left a light on in the family room all night. These examples help me see a bit more clearly what Anselm meant.

When I noticed these minor acts of neglect, I found myself apologizing. Each one felt like a bigger deal than the next, and I began keeping a mental tally of my faults. I felt so rotten about it that when I noticed something my spouse had left undone, I jumped on it. I wanted to even the score or cancel out one of my own marks. But how does pointing out the fault in another fix your own? It felt like another point against me. I tried to focus on good deeds around the house, but they couldn't erase the negatives if they were simply what I wanted to achieve in the first place.

The same is true for our relationship with God. We may want to perfectly love and serve God, but it is impossible for us to do so. Sometimes we get lost trying to account for it all. Every sin and every mistake feel like a tally mark on an eternal scorecard. Good deeds can't earn us brownie points with God because they are simply the baseline expectation of how we should live as faithful people. Like that eternal scorecard from the Good Place, it hangs over us, and the shame, guilt, and hopelessness can drag us down even further.

In the Letter to the Colossians, Paul reminds us that if we live according to this scorecard, we are dead already (2:13). The very life is sucked out of us in this eternal striving for an unattainable goal. But why are we keeping score? Why do we let that narrative of our mistakes capture our attention and hold us back?

Christmas, in fact the whole Christian life, offers us a different narrative. It gives us the good news that Christ has come, and that has made all the difference for our present and our future. As Colossians goes on to say, we have been made alive in Christ. He has wiped the slate clean and blotted out all of the handwriting of our misdeeds (2:14). All of those expectations and guilt and the record of our imperfections were taken away. They are no more.

In my marriage, I had to learn to trust that my spouse was with me not because I did everything the right way. I was loved, and I loved him, and there was no need to keep track of our mistakes. As Paul tells us, we shouldn't be distracted by those expectations. "Just go ahead with what you've been given. You received Christ Jesus, the Master; now *live* him" (Colossians 2:6-7 MSG). We can stop keeping score. After all, God has.

*Rev. Katie Z. Dawson*

# Do I feel the assurance that I have been redeemed of my sins?

Have you heard the story of the mischievous little boy who wants a little brother for Christmas? He was about eight years old and decided the best strategy for achieving his goal is to write a letter to God pleading his case.

First Draft: *"Dear God, I really want a little brother and I'm always good, so. . . ."* No, that wasn't quite right. He wasn't always good and God was sure to know it. So he crumpled the paper and began again.

Second Draft: *"Dear God, I really want a little brother and since I'm good most of the time. . . ."* That wasn't exactly true either. His past behavior presented a challenge in making a believable appeal. He crumpled up that letter too and sat down in a quandary.

As he wrestled with his problem, his eye caught the family nativity set displayed on the table. With a flash of inspiration, he dashed out of the room and returned with a white linen napkin. Very gently, he lifted the little ceramic figure of Mary from the manger scene and carefully wrapped her in the linen cloth. Placing the wrapped figure in front of him, he eagerly started a new letter.

*"Dear God, if you ever want to see your Mother again. . . ."* Ha!

Maybe this is an extreme example, but we've all probably done something like this before where we tried to negotiate with God. Sometimes we beg, sometimes we promise, sometimes we plead, and sometimes we bargain, trying to convince God to do something based on our merit or promises of future goodness. However, these things don't work. Not because God is unreachable or unpleasable or doesn't care about our requests. No, these things don't work because God doesn't work like that! And when we resort to such things, it shows that we really do not have a clear understanding of God at all.

Here are the facts:

1. You can't cajole, bribe, manipulate, or sweet-talk God into doing things for you.
2. You don't have to.

Some years ago, Andy Stanley wrote a little book called *How Good Is Good Enough?* The premise of the book is that none of us can be good enough to earn God's attention, grace, or love. No one. But the good news is, we don't have to. Jesus did that for us. What we cannot earn, Jesus gives us as a gift—salvation, forgiveness, adoption, and friendship with God.

Please don't misunderstand or get the wrong impression about God. He's not an old curmudgeon that Jesus has to convince to tolerate us. No. We were separated from God by our sin. So God made a plan. He would rescue us, atone for us, and bring us back to God, by the sacrificial death of his Son Jesus.

If we seek assurance that we have been redeemed of our sins, we need look no further than the sacrifice of Christ and our experience of this gift of salvation.

John Wesley preached a sermon about "the almost Christian"—people going through the motions but lacking a depth of faith and love in their heart. I have to wonder if "almost Christians" are implicitly trying to earn favor with God by being nice instead of trusting wholly in the life, death, and resurrection of Jesus. I suppose some people have an "almost Christmas" too. Sometimes we go through the motions. We wrap the presents. We decorate the tree. But friends, please don't miss Jesus. He loves you. God loves you! Christmas is about God sending his son on a rescue mission. We were the hostages and Jesus came to set us free, to save us, to forgive us, to adopt us into his family and give us a new relationship with God. Do you feel the assurance of that? Do you feel it as a free gift, not something to be earned but something already received, something to be celebrated?

The little boy writing the letter to God missed it. He did not yet understand how much God loves him. I hope you don't miss Christmas this year. God loves you! Jesus came on a rescue mission so that you can be accepted and loved and adopted and forgiven. Merry Rescue Mission!

*Rev. Jim Cowart*

# Do I feel the assurance of the Spirit that I am a child of God?

There are so many decisions to make every day. Some decisions seem to have some hefty consequences, while others are so small our brain barely registers that we've made a decision at all! It's estimated that, based on impulsive and logical thinking, the average adult makes around thirty-five thousand decisions each day. As a parent of three little human beings, I find that my need to make more decisions seems to have grown exponentially. I remember when they were babies and looking down at them while they slept so peacefully and calmly. As their eyes fluttered with dreams and involuntary smiles crept across their faces, I would allow my thoughts to wander to all the decisions that they would face. We live in a world that contains so much turmoil and access and so many choices that I couldn't even conceive of what they would face. Yet, with all that was running through my mind, I would look down and see their eyes flutter and wonder if they had any idea how I desperately wanted to create a way for them in the world. I wonder if this is the same way that Mary looked at Jesus as she held him as a wiggly, squirmy infant?

As my kids have grown up, our relationship has changed. They no longer snooze in my arms with their sleepy eyelids fluttering while in dreamland. Times of tantrums, disobedience, and independence have also entered into our routine. They don't behave perfectly (nor do I). They push boundaries trying to discover where I end and they begin, and sometimes they are downright disagreeable (as am I). But there is one thing that has been our constant through these years: love.

If we've had a particularly hard day, it is not unusual for one of them to find me later after the tears have dried and the dust has settled and say, "Momma, I'm sorry for what happened. Do you still love me?"

This question without fail takes my breath away. My first thought always is, how could they think there is anything they could do that would make me stop loving them? My second thought is, I'm a failure of a parent if they don't know I will love them no matter what! And usually, my third thought is, this is the same love God has for me. Nothing they could do would make me decide to stop loving them. This is when I feel the assurance that I am a child of God. There is nothing that we can do to separate ourselves from God's love for us.

When we look at our own and others' decisions, it can be really easy to hold up a critical lens and see all the mishaps and mistakes we've made. We judge our mistakes through our human understanding, assigning our worth based on whether we are "good" or "bad." But Paul helps us see the depths of God's love in Romans 8:38-39 (NLT):

*And I am convinced that nothing can ever separate us from God's love. Neither death nor life, neither angels nor demons, neither our fears for today nor our worries about tomorrow—not even the powers of hell can separate us from God's love. No power in the sky above or in the earth below—indeed, nothing in all creation will ever be able to separate us from the love of God that is revealed in Christ Jesus our Lord.*

I am blown away time and time again by how often I underestimate God's love for me. Not only does God love me completely, with my bad mistakes and bad decisions, and without restriction, God loves each and every one of us deeply and completely. We are children of God. People I struggle with, God loves. People I disagree with, God loves. People who challenge, God loves. God loves them completely with mistakes and bad decisions, and without restriction. Not only does the thought of this take my breath away, it moves me to tears. I am a beloved child of God, and so are you. God's love for me is deeper than my comprehension of love, and for that I am truly grateful. May we feel the assurance that we are children of God!

*Rev. Kim Montenegro*

Can I lift my hand up to heaven,
and declare to him that
lives forever and ever,
"Lord, You know all things.
You know that I love You"?

Psalm 139 (NRSV) begins with, "O LORD, you have searched me and known me" (verse 1). God knows us better than we know ourselves, and the good news is that God still bothers to be our God. The writer goes on: "Even before a word is on my tongue, O LORD, you know it completely" (verse 4). If God knows everything that we are going to say or do, some might ask, "Then what's the point?" Why pray? Why seek God's guidance or express our desires? Some may hear this psalm as an expression of God's glory, power, and magnificence, but I think a better reading of this familiar psalm is as an expression of God's patience and grace. It's humbling to hear that God knows what we are going to say, and yet God has the patience to listen anyway. It is a knowledge that certainly surpasses my understanding for God to know and search me and continue to covenant with me on the way that leads to life. God may indeed know what we are going to pray before we have the courage to form our words, but God is not a manager who is interested in the daily report. God is fundamentally interested in you. Think of it this way. Every morning before leaving for the office, I always tell my wife "I love you." Saying "I love you" is not a conveyance of information; rather it is an investment in relationship.

The psalm continues with, "For it was you who formed my inward parts; you knit me together in my mother's womb. I praise you, for I am fearfully and wonderfully made" (verses 13-14). I invite you for a moment to hear this psalm from Jesus' lips. Christmas is a celebration remembering that God put on flesh and was born to show us what God's love is. Hearing this psalm as part of Jesus' praise offers a beautiful and haunting frame through which to hear these words to God. "Where can I go from your spirit . . . if I make my bed in Sheol, you are there . . . even the darkness is not dark to you. . . . In your book were written all the days that were formed for me" (verses 7, 8, 12, 16). Could it be that this psalm was part of Jesus' devotion, so private that not even the Gospel writers knew to record it?

What does it mean to you that God knows all things and remains in a loving and covenantal relationship with us? Although this is an Easter story, this psalm reminds me of when Jesus met Peter on the lakeshore after the Resurrection. Jesus is standing around a charcoal fire, similar to the fire around which Peter had stood denying that he knew Jesus. In other words, Jesus knew. Jesus knew and appropriately asked Peter, "Do you love me?" Three times he asks, which may seem heavy-handed or abrasive, until we take a step back and recognize that Jesus is offering forgiveness for each time Peter denied him. Near the end of the story Peter seems offended and replies, "Lord, you know I love you" (John 21:15, 16, 17). Of course Jesus knew that, but sometimes we just have to say it out loud, and often more than once. The exchange between Jesus and Peter was not about sharing information; rather it was about the kind of love and patient grace God has for us in the person of Jesus.

The Lord searches us and knows all things, and yet still invites us into the life of God. May we declare, "You know that I love you!"

*Rev. Matt Rawle*

## *Hymn Reflection*:
## "Come, Let Us Anew Our Journey Pursue"

At the end of the year, many of us will just roll right on through; we'll celebrate with fireworks or noisemakers and never look back. A few of us will take a moment to review the twelve months prior, and we might remember the "best of" moments, compiling them into a "Top 9" Instagram post or including them in a holiday letter to family and friends. We might take time to recall holidays and vacations, birthdays and awards, as well as lost loved ones and difficult trials persevered.

But how often do we inventory the prior year in terms of God's call on our lives? How often do we offer the prior year to God and try to see it through God's eyes? What if we were able to hear from God, "Well done, good and faithful servant"? What if God could gently show us the opportunities in which we might have shared love or taught peace but didn't, as encouragement and challenge for the future? What if God could point out the times that we allowed ourselves to be conduits of the Spirit, allowing deeper discipleship and even transformation to occur as a result, helping us to see the ways we've been faithful, and the ways that have made a difference in the world?

In Charles Wesley's hymn, "Come, Let Us Anew Our Journey Pursue," he wrote:

> *O that each in the day of His coming may say,*
> *"I have fought my way through; . . .*
> *I have finished the work thou didst give me to do!"*
> *O that each from his Lord may receive the glad word,*
> *"Well and faithfully done! . . .*
> *Enter into my joy, and sit down on my throne!"*[1]

Perhaps that might be the hope with which we look back on this past year: that we might be able to say, "I did the work God gave me to do," and we might each hear from God, "Well done—now enter into my joy." What a gift that would be! Take time today to examine the year just past for joys and sorrows, for faithfulness and missed opportunities, and offer it all to God, listening for God's response and encouragement.

And at the same time, for most of us, the end of the calendar year is not the end of the work God has given us to do for our lives. So in addition to looking back at how and when we've served God in the past year, today is also a time to look forward and ask God for the strength, humility, and conviction to love and serve God fully in the year ahead. Earlier in Wesley's hymn, he wrote:

> *Come, let us anew our journey pursue,*
> *Roll round with the year, . . .*
> *And never stand still till the Master appear.*
> *His adorable will let us gladly fulfill,*
> *And our talents improve, . . .*
> *By the patience of hope, and the labor of love.*

As we look ahead into the new year, might this be our prayer, as well? Take time today to pray that you will continue to pursue this journey with God, this journey of discipleship, this journey of the "altogether Christian"; that you will love God with heart and mind and soul and strength and love your neighbor as yourself. Take time to pray for God's guidance in the new year, that by following in the way of Jesus this year, you might experience holy freedom, rejoice in the hope and peace that only God gives, and share the love of God with everyone you encounter. Then you'll be sure to hear, at the end of this next year, "Well and faithfully done . . . enter into my joy!"

*Rev. Elizabeth Ingram Schindler*

1 Charles Wesley, "Come, Let Us Anew Our Journey Pursue," Hymnary.org, accessed July 17, 2019, https://hymnary.org/text/come_let_us_anew_our _journey_pursue_roll.

## 31

## "I am no longer my own"

On this New Year's Eve, as you look back at the year behind you and anticipate the one before you, you would do well to ponder this important question:

"Who am I? What am I supposed to be?"

That's the question that plagued an Indian man in Saudi Arabia in October 2013, after he appeared in front of the Indian Consulate, unconscious. When he was finally revived in a private hospital, he could not recall his name, hometown, or passport particulars. He was diagnosed with a brain tumor that caused significant memory loss. In short, he did not know who he was.

A charitable agency began working with government officials to help establish his identity. They posted his picture on social media and within a few short months, thousands had seen his picture. Someone finally recognized him. Officials contacted his wife, who was overjoyed to learn that he was found. She provided documentation to prove his identity: Dhanigaivel Gunasekaran. When reporters showed up to interview Mr. Gunasekaran in the hospital, they found him weeping with tears of joy and relief in his hospital bed.[1]

There is nothing like discovering who you really are. These are questions that lie at the deepest level of our existence. "Who am I and why am I here?" "What defines me?" "What am I supposed to be?"

Oh, if only these questions were merely about what career to pursue, or where to live, or whom to marry. They're not. The questions are much deeper than that. They're about identity and purpose.

They're questions that we ask in our middle-aged years, as we pass the halfway point in our lives, wondering how differently we might live the second act of life compared to the first.

They're questions that haunt us in our private moments when we struggle with how our public persona matches our essential self.

They're questions that comprise our truest personality, our personal history, our values, our uniqueness as a person, and, especially, our relationship to God.

And they're questions that are appropriate to ask as we conclude our Christmas journey and look ahead to the new year.

So, it should be no wonder that for generations, Methodists have begun the new year with the Wesley Covenant Prayer, which offers a clear, succinct answer to the question, "Who am I? What am I supposed to be?"

> *"I am no longer my own, but thine."*[2]

With all the ways that our culture would want to define you, and how you may have struggled to find out who you really are, you need only remember this: you belong to God.

You belong to God, even when you question what God is calling you to do, or whom God has placed in your life ("Put me to what thou wilt, rank me with whom thou wilt").

You belong to God, even when life takes a wrong turn. ("Put me to doing, put me to suffering").

You belong to God, even when you're not sure if you are doing God's will, or hearing God at all ("Let me be employed by thee or laid aside for thee").

You belong to God, even when you feel on top of the world, or when it feels like your faith has cost you dearly ("exalted for thee or brought low for thee").

You belong to God, even when you feel content, or when you are longing to fill a void ("Let me be full, let me be empty").

You belong to God, even if you have it all, or when you have nothing at all ("Let me have all things, let me have nothing").

So that leaves only one true and right response: Surrender. Render all of yourself into the glory and blessing of God and remember that no matter what, "thou art mine, and I am thine."

And let that conviction remind you of who you are and guide you into the year ahead.

*Rev. Magrey R. deVega*

1  PTI, "Facebook Helps Establish Identity of Indian in Saudi Arabia," *The Economic Times*, updated December 17, 2013, https://economictimes.indiatimes.com/nri/nris-in-news/facebook-helps-establish-identity-of-indian-in-saudi-arabia/articleshow/27527096.cms.

2  "A Covenant Prayer in the Wesleyan Tradition," *The United Methodist Hymnal* (Nashville, TN: The United Methodist Publishing House, 1989), 607.

# Almost Christmas

A Wesleyan Advent Experience

Almost Christmas
978-1-5018-9057-4

Almost Christmas: DVD
978-1-5018-9062-8

Almost Christmas: Leader Guide
978-1-5018-9060-4

Almost Christmas: Youth Study Book
978-1-5018-9067-3

Almost Christmas: Devotions
978-1-5018-9069-7

---

Also from Magrey R. deVega
*Awaiting the Already*
*Embracing the Uncertain*

Also from Matt Rawle
*The Redemption of Scrooge*
*The Gift of the Nutcracker*
*What Makes a Hero?*
*The Grace of Les Misérables*

CPSIA information can be obtained
at www.ICGtesting.com
Printed in the USA
LVHW011951121119
637170LV00004B/4/P